Learn to Code

Practice Book 3

Written by

Claire Lotriet

Published by

RISING STARS

The Publishers would like to thank the following for permission to reproduce copyright material.

Acknowledgements

Photos: Pages 1–3, 5–7, 9–11,13–15: screenshots from Kodu Game Lab, from FUSE Labs, Microsoft Research; pages 17–19, 21–23, 25–27, 29–31: screenshots from Snap!: Snap! was written by Jens Mönig and is distributed by the University of California, Berkeley. It is licensed under the GNU Affero General Public License (https://www.gnu.org/licenses/agpl); pages 33–35, 37–39, 41–43, 45–47: screenshots from MSW Logo, developed by softronix (http://www.softronix.com/logo. html). All used with permission.

Every effort has been made to trace all copyright holders, but if any have been inadvertently overlooked, the Publishers will be pleased to make the necessary arrangements at the first opportunity.

Rising Stars is grateful for the following people and their schools who contributed to the development of these materials: Matt Rogers, Snowsfields Primary School; Dawn Hallybone, Oakdale Junior School; Marc Faulder, Burton Joyce Primary School; Martyn Soulsby, North Lakes School; John Janowski, Royal Russell Junior School.

Although every effort has been made to ensure that website addresses are correct at time of going to press, Rising Stars cannot be held responsible for the content of any website mentioned in this book. It is sometimes possible to find a relocated web page by typing in the address of the home page for a website in the URL window of your browser.

Hachette UK's policy is to use papers that are natural, renewable and recyclable products and made from wood grown in well-managed forests and other controlled sources. The logging and manufacturing processes are expected to conform to the environmental regulations of the country of origin.

Orders: please contact Hachette UK Distribution, Hely Hutchinson Centre, Milton Road, Didcot, Oxfordshire, OX11 7HH. Telephone: (44) 01235 400555. Email primary@hachette.co.uk

Lines are open from 9 a.m. to 5 p.m., Monday to Saturday, with a 24-hour message answering service. Visit our website at www.risingstars-uk.com for details of the full range of Rising Starspublications.

Online support and queries email: onlinesupport@risingstars-uk.com

ISBN: 978 1 7833 9343 5

Publisher: Becca Law
Computing consultant: Miles Berry
Text design and typesetting: Words and Pictures Ltd, London
Cover design: Burville-Riley Partnership
Editorial: Jenny Draine
Project manager: Estelle Lloyd
Illustrations: Eva Sassin, Advocate Art

A catalogue record for this title is available from the British Library.

Contents

How to use this book

Learning to code can seem like learning a new language! This book will show you how to code using three different tools. You will make your own games, procedures and a text-to-Morse-code converter!

The step-by-step instructions explain what you need to do.

8 Next we need to add on the Unicode of the next character in the text. To do this, click on the `Operators` palette and insert a `Unicode of …` block into the `add thing to … Unicode` block where it says *thing*. Then snap a `letter 1 of world` block into the box that says *a*. Snap in an orange `i` variable where it says *1* and `text` parameter where it says *world*.

This text shows the words you'll see on the screen.

9 Now snap the `report` block back onto the end of the script and snap a `Unicode` variable inside it. Then click `OK`.

This is needed because we want to tell the function to report a list of Unicode back. The user could type in text and get a list of Unicode back.

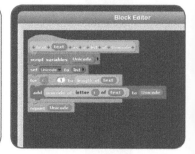

Handy tips give you extra help.

10 To test your function you need to add the new block to the scripting area, so click on the `Operators` palette and drag a `text … as a list of Unicode` block into the scripting area. Type some text into the block. Try **hello**.

Remember we set the input as text. If your function works correctly, what should the output be?

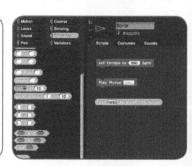

This text shows what you need to type in.

11 Finally, click on the `text … as a list of Unicode` block to run it. It should convert the text you typed into Unicode. Be sure to save your project again.

Remember Unicode is what computers use to represent letters. We can see that a lower case 'h' is 104 in Unicode and so on. The output produced by your function is Unicode.

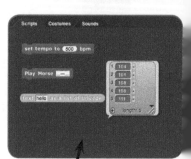

This text shows the commands you need to use in the program.

The pictures show what you should see on your screen.

This book uses three tools: Kodu, Logo and Snap!. Work your way through the activities for each tool in order. Each activity builds on the previous one.

Now try this...

- Can you type **HELLO** in upper case into your block? What do you notice about the Unicode? Do upper and lower case letters have the same Unicode number? How are these related?

- Can you type more than one word with spaces in between into your block? What is the Unicode number for a space?

- Can you find out the Unicode numbers for all letters of the alphabet?

- How are numbers and other characters, like non-Latin alphabets, represented in Unicode?

- How quickly can you convert words in text to their equivalents in Unicode?

Take your learning further by trying these extra challenges!

These activities help you develop your understanding of coding away from the computer.

Key words

Can you explain to a partner what these words mean?

function   input   output   variable   list   parameter   Unicode

These are important words that you need to understand. You can find definitions in the glossary on page 56.

How did you do?

Think about what you did in this activity. Did you:

- build a block that converts text into Unicode?
- explore upper case and lower case letters in Unicode?
- find out how a space is represented in Unicode?
- find out the Unicode numbers for the whole alphabet?
- explore how numbers are represented in Unicode?

Use these questions to review what you have learned in the activity.

47

Top tips

Writing code to make something happen is exciting, but sometimes your code won't work as well as it could, or it won't work at all!

What happens when your code doesn't do what you want it to? You need to fix it!

The process of making our code better, or correcting mistakes (removing bugs in the code) is called debugging.

If you find a problem with your code, try to solve it yourself first, before asking a grown-up. The coding monsters are here to help you!

When you have finished writing your code, always run your program or script to see if it works.

Go through your code step by step in your head. Try to predict what will happen. Can you spot any mistakes?

for coding

Try explaining each bit of your code to a partner. Does it all make sense?

Try explaining your code to a rubber duck. Rubber duck debugging is used by proper programmers to fix errors in their code!

Show your code to a partner. Do they have any ideas about how to fix code that isn't working?

Activity 1: Kodu Programming how characters move

Kodu allows you to build a computer game in your own virtual world. First you need to decide how the user will control Kodu, the main character. Work through the steps below to program different keys to move Kodu in different ways.

1

Kodu can be downloaded at **www.kodugamelab.com**. Start by clicking on `New world` in the main menu. It will open a new, empty world where your game will take place. Press the `Page Up` key to zoom in on the terrain (the ground).

> Make sure `Num Lock` is off before using the `Page Up` key to zoom in.

2

Now click on the `Object` tool in the menu along the bottom of the screen. The `Object` tool looks like Kodu. This allows you to add or edit characters and objects. Click somewhere on the terrain to bring up the pie menu. Click on `Kodu` to add the Kodu character to your world.

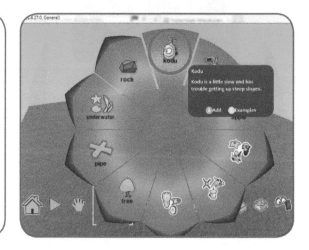

3

Hover over Kodu to bring up a menu of different-coloured discs. Use the `right arrow` key to move along the menu to change Kodu's colour to blue.

> You can change the colour of any character or object in this way.

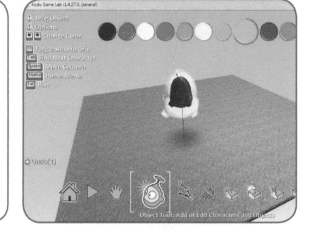

4

Right-click on Kodu to bring up another menu of options. Click on the one at the top, `Program`. This will take you into the programming screen.

> Right-clicking on any object brings up a menu of options.

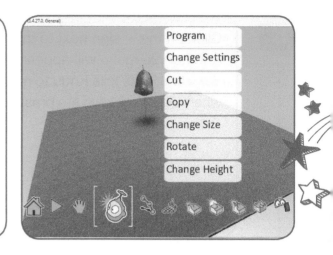

5

Now you can see a programming box with *WHEN* and *DO* boxes in it. Click on the + sign next to the *WHEN* box, then `keyboard`.

> Programming in Kodu is based on 'when' and 'do' instructions. For example, you tell Kodu: 'When this happens, I want you to do this'.

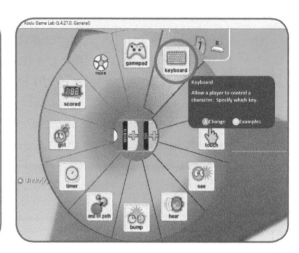

6

You should see a *keyboard* tile in the *WHEN* box. Click on the + sign next to the *keyboard* tile to bring up another pie menu. Click on `Arrows`. There should now be a *keyboard* and an *arrows* tile in the *WHEN* box.

> Your user will input control of Kodu by using the arrow keys on the keyboard.

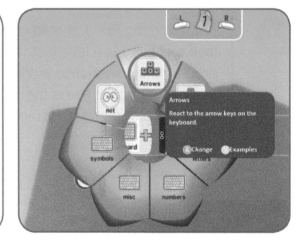

7

Click on the + sign next to the *DO* box. This brings up another pie menu. Click on `move`. There should now be a *move* tile in the *DO* box.

> If you make a mistake and add the wrong tile at any point, just right-click on the tile and click on `Cut Tile` to remove it.

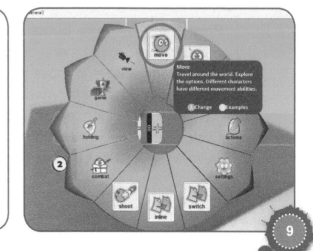

8

Click on the + sign next to the *move* tile. Another pie menu will appear. Click on `forward`. This tells Kodu to move forward when the arrow keys are pressed.

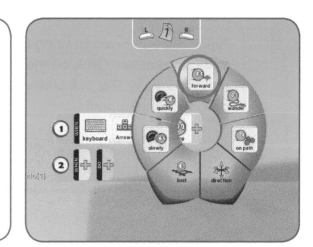

9

Now click on the + sign next to the *forward* tile to bring up another pie menu. Click on `slowly`. This tile tells Kodu to move slowly.

> You can use several *slowly* tiles to make Kodu move even slower.

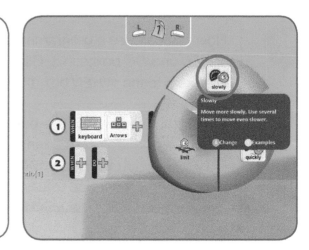

10

Programming row 1 should look like this (see picture). Now let's test whether the programming sequence works and if it needs debugging. Press the `Esc` key to leave the programming screen.

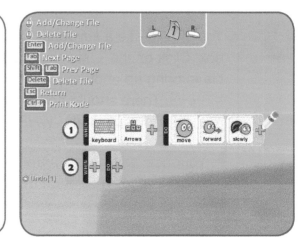

11

Press the `Play Game` button (the large green triangle) in the menu at the bottom. Use the arrow keys to move Kodu around your terrain. To exit play mode when you have finished testing, press `Esc` again. Click on the `Home Menu` button and then `Save my world` to save your game so far.

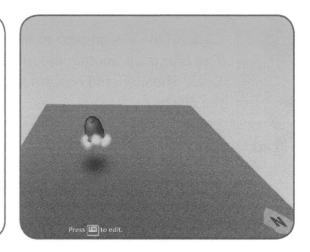

Now try this . . .

- Can you change Kodu from blue to another colour?

- Can you change the tiles so Kodu wanders randomly rather than moving forward when the arrow keys are pressed?

- Can you change the *WHEN* box so the user controls Kodu by pressing the W, A, S and D keys instead of the arrow keys?

- Can you change the speed at which Kodu moves when the keys are pressed?

 Work in pairs: one person should act as Kodu and the other should be the person playing the game. Instruct your partner to move in different directions and in different ways around the room.

Key words

Can you explain to a partner what these words mean?

program   **when**   **do**   **input**   **debug**

How did you do?

Think about what you did in this activity. Did you:

- create a game that allows a user to control Kodu using the arrow keys on their keyboard?

- change Kodu's colour?

- change the direction in which Kodu moves?

- change the keys with which the user controls Kodu?

- change the speed at which Kodu moves?

Activity 2: Kodu Programming characters to collect objects

You have programmed Kodu to move when the arrow keys are pressed. Now you can think about how your game will work. In this activity you will program Kodu to eat different objects.

1

Start by loading the world you created in activity 1. Click on `Load world` in the main menu and then `My Worlds`. Click on your world and then `Edit` in the menu that appears.

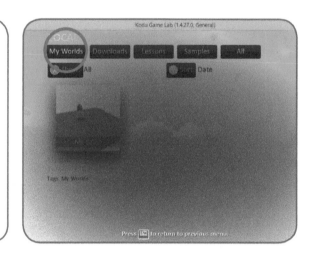

2

We need to add some more terrain so Kodu has more ground to move about on. Press the `Page Down` key to zoom out. Click on the `Ground Brush` tool in the menu along the bottom. Now click where you want to add new terrain.

Right-click on any pieces of terrain you want to delete.

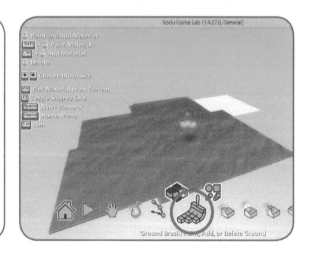

3

Now it's time to add some objects. Click on the `Object` tool in the menu along the bottom. Then click anywhere on the terrain. Click on the `objects` section of the pie menu. The objects section in the pie menu has a picture of a rocket, castle and coin on it. Click on `star`. Repeat this three times so there are three stars in your world.

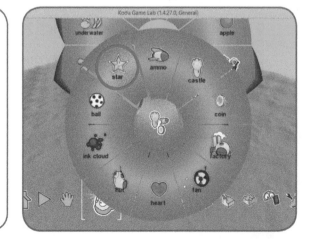

4

Right-click on Kodu and click on `Program` in the menu. On row 2 of the program, click on the + sign next to the *WHEN* box and then on `see`. Now click on the + sign next to the *see* tile. In the pie menu, click on `objects` and then on `more`. Finally click on `star`.

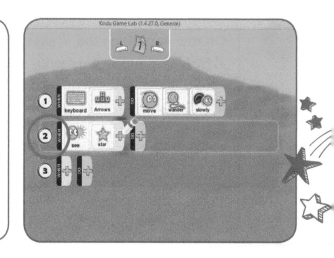

5

Click on the + sign next to the *DO* box and click on `actions`. Then click on `express`. Click on the + sign next to the *express* tile. Click on `stars` in the pie menu.

> When Kodu sees a star, stars will move around his head. This could show your user when they are near an object for scoring points.

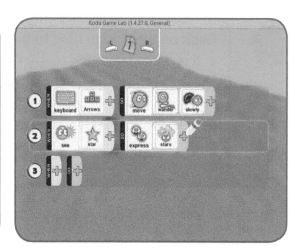

6

On program row 3, click on the + sign next to the *WHEN* box and then on `bump` in the pie menu. Now click on the + sign next to the *bump* tile. In the pie menu, click on `objects` and then on `more`. Finally click on `star`.

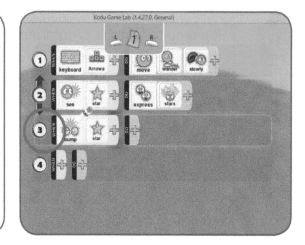

7

Now click on the + sign next to the *DO* box and click on `eat`. Then click on the + sign next to the *eat* tile and click on `it`.

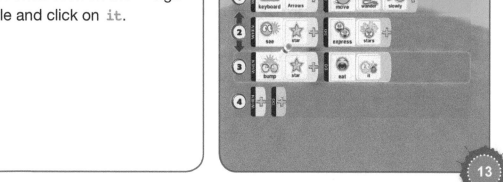

8 On row 4, click on the + sign next to the *WHEN* box. In the pie menu, click on `see`. Now click on the + sign next to the *see* tile and click on `objects`, then `more`, then `star`.

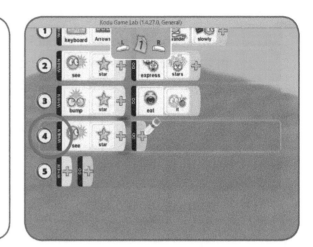

9 Click on the + sign next to the *DO* box and, in the pie menu, click `move`. Click on the + sign next to the *move* tile and click `toward` in the pie menu. Finally, click on the + sign next to the *toward* tile and click `quickly`.

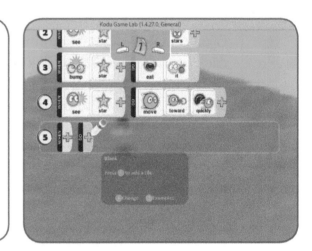

10 It's time to test the programming sequences you have created and see if the programming needs debugging. Press the `Esc` key. Then click on the `Play Game` icon in the menu.

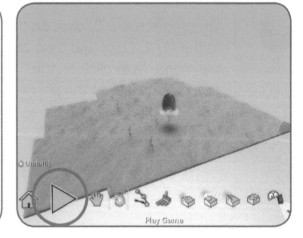

11 In play mode, watch as Kodu spots the three stars you placed on the terrain. He glows with stars, then moves towards them and eats them. Press `Esc` when you have finished. Don't forget to click on the `Home menu` icon and then click `Save my world` to save your progress.

Now try this . . .

- Can you change the objects Kodu eats to something other than stars?

- Can you change how Kodu reacts to the stars when he sees them?

- Can you change what Kodu does when he bumps into a star?

- Can you make Kodu glow a different colour when he eats a star?

 Create a 'when and do' Kodu programming sequence for a partner and challenge them to explain to you what will happen in play mode. Were they right?

Key words

Can you explain to a partner what these words mean?

program   **action**   **consequence**   **debug**

How did you do?

Think about what you did in this activity. Did you:

- program Kodu to react to the stars, move towards them and eat them?

- try adding some other objects for Kodu to eat other than stars?

- change your code so Kodu expresses he is happy in another way other than glowing stars?

- program Kodu so he doesn't eat the stars when he bumps into them but does something else instead?

- program Kodu to glow a different colour upon eating a star?

Activity 3: Kodu
Programming objects to move

To make your game more interesting, you can add other objects to your world and make them move in different ways. Work your way through the steps below to explore programming objects to move randomly or follow motion paths.

1 Start by loading the world you created and saved in the previous activity. Click on `Load world` in the main menu and then `My Worlds`. Click on your world and then `Edit` in the menu that appears.

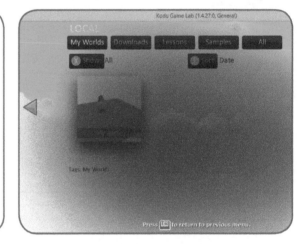

2 Click on the `Object` tool and then click somewhere on the terrain. On the pie menu, click on the section underneath the *apple* section. Then click on `balloon`.

> If the balloon is too large, right-click on it and click on `change size` in the menu. Drag the slider to the left to make it smaller. All objects can be resized in this way.

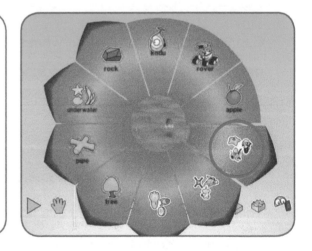

3 Right-click on the balloon and then click on `Program` to go to the programming screen. On row 1, click on the + sign next to the *WHEN* box. In the pie menu, click on `more`. Then click on `always`.

4

Click on the + sign next to the *DO* box and click on `move` in the pie menu. Click on the + sign next to the *move* tile and click on `wander` in the pie menu. Finally, click the + sign next to the *wander* tile and click on `slowly` in the pie menu. Press the `Esc` key. Right-click on the balloon and click on `Copy`.

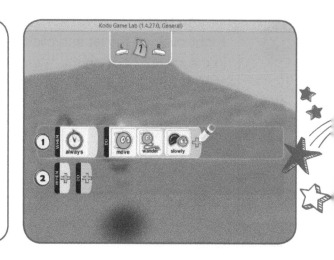

5

Right-click somewhere else on the terrain and click on `paste` to paste another balloon into your world. Repeat this again so you have three balloons in total.

> When you copy and paste an object, it also copies and pastes its programming sequences so it will behave in the same way as the original object.

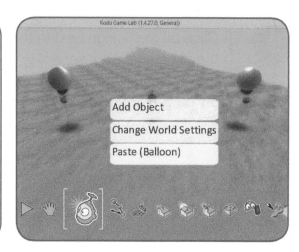

6

Click on the `Move Camera` tool (it looks like a hand). Hold right-click on the mouse and rotate the terrain so you are looking at it from above. Click on the `Path` tool (next to the *Object* tool). Click on the terrain to place a point. Keep doing this to create a path around your world. Double-click on the first point to end the path.

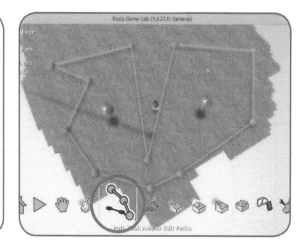

7

Click on the `Object` tool again and then click on the terrain. In the pie menu, click on the section underneath the *apple* section. Then click on `jet`.

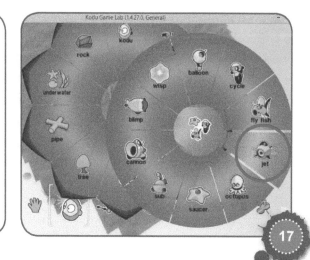

8 Right-click on the jet and click on `Program` in the menu. Click on the + sign next to the *WHEN* box. In the pie menu, click on `more` and then `always`.

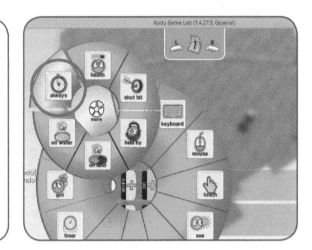

9 Click on the + sign next to the *DO* box. In the pie menu, click on `move`. Then click on the + sign next to the *move* tile and click on `on path`. Press the `Esc` key.

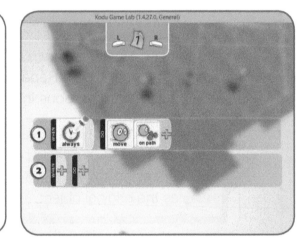

10 Now you can test how the objects move and whether the programming sequences need debugging. Click on the `Play Game` icon to enter play mode.

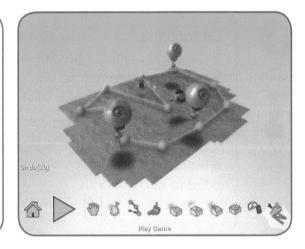

11 In play mode, watch as the jet moves along the path you have created and the three balloons move over the terrain randomly. Objects moving around in different ways make the game less predictable for the player. Press `Esc` when you are finished. Remember to click on the `Home Menu` icon and then `Save my world` to save your progress.

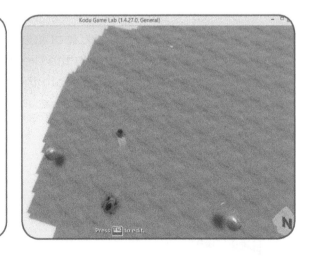

Now try this . . .

- Can you change how quickly the balloons move about?

- Can you change how quickly the jet follows the path?

- Can you change the script so the balloons only start moving when Kodu bumps into them?

- Can you add another path and program a different object, like a blimp, to follow it?

 Create a map of your classroom and different paths to show how you move around it to get to different places. Compare your paths with a partner. Whose path is the shortest? How many different paths can you find to get from your seat to the door? Remember that different algorithms can solve the same problem or perform the same task.

Key words

Can you explain to a partner what these words mean?

program   **debug**   **path**   **test**

How did you do?

Think about what you did in this activity. Did you:

- program balloons that move randomly and a jet that moves along a given path?

- make the balloons move at different speeds?

- change the script so the jet follows the path at a different speed?

- change the script so the balloons only start to move when Kodu bumps into them?

- add in a second object that follows a different path?

Activity 4: Kodu
Programming a points system

Now you need to think about how your user can score points. Work through the steps below to program Kodu to score points in different ways, such as eating certain objects or firing at other objects. You can award a different number of points to different objects too.

1 Start by loading the world you created and saved in the previous activity. Click on `Load world` in the main menu and then `My Worlds`. Click on your world and then `Edit` in the menu that appears.

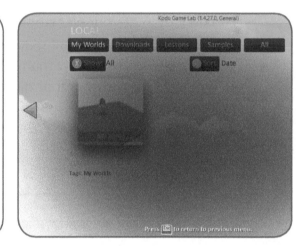

2 Click on the `Object` tool and then right-click on the Kodu character on the terrain and select `Program`. On row 5, click on the + sign in the *WHEN* box. In the pie menu, click on `keyboard`. Then click on the + sign next to the *keyboard* tile and click on `letters`. Then click on `more` and finally the letter `M`.

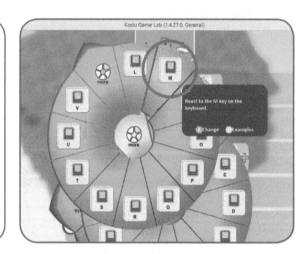

3 Click on the + sign next to the *DO* box. Click on `shoot`. Then click on the next + sign and click on `direction` and then `up`. Finally, click on the + sign next to the *up* tile and select `blip`.

This means when the *M* key is pressed, Kodu will shoot a blip upwards. The user could score points by targeting the blip at certain objects.

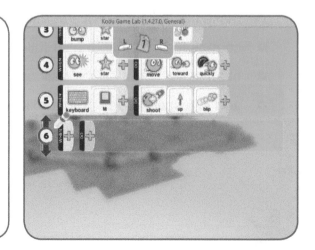

4

On row 6, click on the + sign in the *WHEN* box. In the pie menu, click on `more` and then `shot hit`. Click on the + sign next to the *shot hit* tile, click on `bots 1` and then `balloon`. Next click on the + sign in the *DO* box. In the pie menu, click on `game` and then `score`.

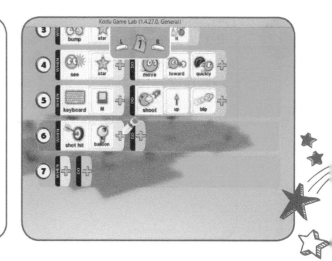

5

Click on the + sign next to the *score* tile and click on `5 points`. Finally, click on the + sign next to the *5 points* tile and click on `scores` and then `green`. This means that when a balloon is hit, the user will score 5 points and this will appear in green.

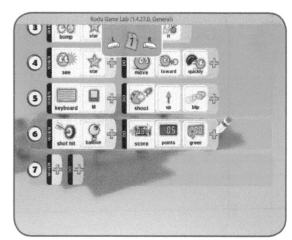

6

Now move on to row 7. Click on the + sign in the *WHEN* box. In the pie menu, click on `more` and then `shot hit`. Click on the + sign next to the *shot hit* tile, click on `bots 1` and then `jet`.

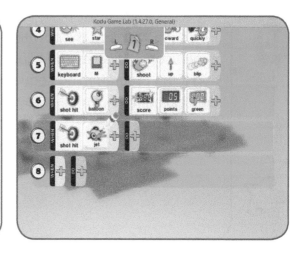

7

Click on the + sign in the *DO* box. In the pie menu, click on `game` and then `score`. Now click on the + sign next to the *score* tile and click on `10 points`. Click on the + sign next to the *10 points* tile and click on `scores` and then `blue`. When a jet is hit, the user will score 10 points and this will appear in blue.

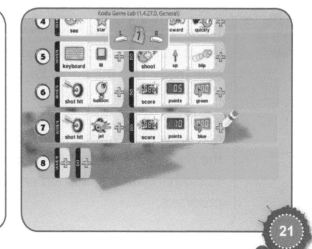

8

It's time to program some points being scored for eating the stars. In the *WHEN* box on row 8, click on the + sign, then `bump`. Click on the + sign next to the *bump* tile, click on `objects`, then `more` and finally `star`.

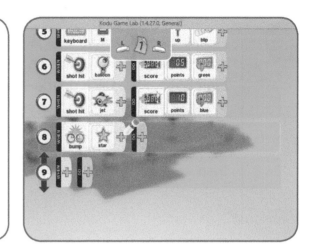

9

Click on the + sign in the *DO* box. In the pie menu, click on `game` and then `score`. Now click on the + sign next to the *score* tile and click on `1 point`. Finally click on the + sign next to the *1 point* tile and click on `scores` and then `pink`.

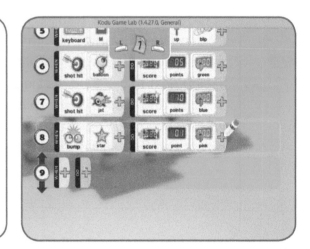

10

Press the `Esc` key. It's now time to check if the scoring system and blip firing works, and if the programming sequence needs debugging. Click on the `Play Game` icon to enter play mode.

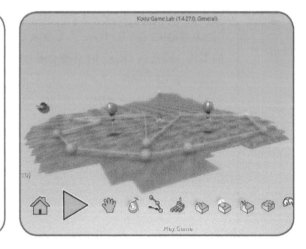

11

Watch carefully as Kodu moves towards the stars and collects one pink point as he eats them. Use the arrow keys to move him around the terrain. When he is underneath a balloon or the jet, press the `M` key to fire a blip upwards. Watch the scores change on the right of the screen. Remember to press `Esc` when you are finished and save your progress.

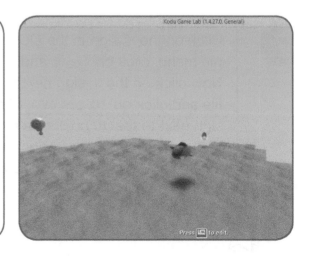

Now try this . . .

- Can you change the points scored for hitting a balloon to 25 and the points for hitting a jet to 30?

- Can you change the script so bumping into certain objects subtracts points from the user's score?

- Can you change the script so hitting a balloon scores you a randomly chosen number of different points each time?

- Can you add another Kodu to make a two-player game?

 Write instructions that tell a new user how to control the different elements of your game and play it.

Key words

Can you explain to a partner what these words mean?

program   **debug**   **user**   **test**

How did you do?

Think about what you did in this activity. Did you:

- program different ways the user can score points?

- change the script so the number of points scored for hitting a balloon or the jet was 25 and 30 instead of 5 and 10?

- change the script so bumping into certain objects subtracts points?

- change the script so hitting a balloon scores a random number of points each time?

- add and program a second Kodu to make a two-player game?

Activity 5: Logo
Writing repetition procedures

Logo is a programming language. It allows you to program a 'turtle' by typing in commands. A 'turtle' is an object on the screen (in this case, a triangle) that draws a 'pen' line behind it, wherever it goes. In this activity you will write programs that draw shapes. You will be using the MSW Logo interpreter.

1

MSWLogo can be downloaded from **www.softronix.com/logo.html**. Start MSWLogo and type **PD** into the *Commander* bar then press the Enter key. Type in **FD 100**. Press Enter. Type **RT 90**. Press Enter.

> PD is short for pen down, FD stands for forward and RT means right turn. The numbers show the number of steps forward and the angle turned.

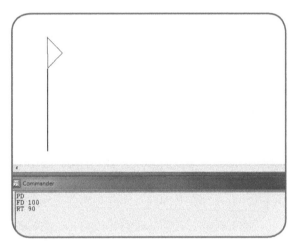

2

Type **FD 100** and press Enter. Type **RT 90** and press Enter. Repeat these commands twice more. The turtle should draw a square.

> You have repeated the same set of commands four times. This means you can use a repetition command to draw a square instead.

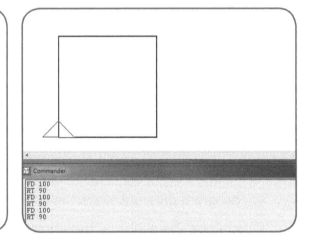

3

Type in **HOME CS** and press Enter. This will reset the turtle and erase the drawing. Now type **REPEAT 4 [FD 100 RT 90]** and press Enter. Any commands in the square brackets will be repeated four times.

> CS stands for clear screen.

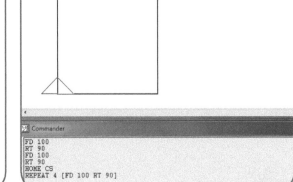

4

Type in **HOME CS** and press Enter.
Now type **REPEAT 3 [FD 100 RT 120]**
and press Enter. This command draws an
equilateral triangle.

> To program in Logo you need to use
> the external angle. You can work this
> out by dividing 360 by the number of
> angles the shape has, e.g. 360 ÷ 3.

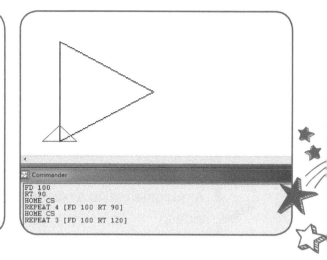

5

Reset the screen (**HOME CS** and Enter).
Let's write the command to draw a regular
pentagon. In the *Commander* bar, type
REPEAT 5 [FD 100 RT 72] and press
Enter.

> To work out the external angle of
> regular polygons, divide 360 by the
> number of angles in the shape, e.g.
> 360 ÷ 5 = 72.

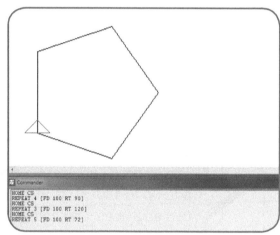

6

Reset the screen (**HOME CS** and Enter).
Type **REPEAT 6 [FD 100 RT 60]** in the
Commander bar. Look at the number of
repetitions (6) and the size of the external
angle. What shape will this command draw?
How do you know? Press Enter to check.

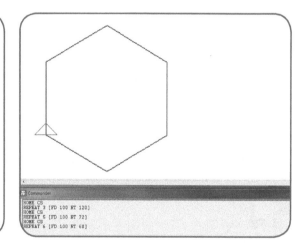

7

Can you now work out the command to
draw a regular octagon?

> Think about how many angles the
> shape has. How can you work out the
> size of its external angles? Look at the
> image if you need more clues.

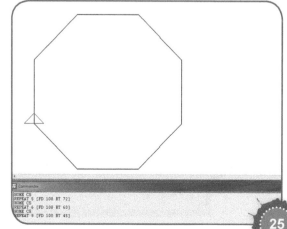

8

Reset the screen (**HOME CS** and **Enter**). It's time to draw some quadrilaterals! Let's start with a rectangle. It will need two sets of repetition because it repeats the long side twice and the short side twice. Type in **REPEAT 2 [FD 100 RT 90 FD 50 RT 90]**. Press **Enter**.

A quadrilateral is a shape with four sides.

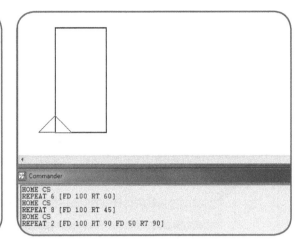

9

The code for drawing a rectangle can be changed to create a parallelogram. A parallelogram also has two long sides and two short sides. Only the angles need changing. Clear the screen as before. Type in **REPEAT 2 [FD 100 RT 45 FD 50 RT 135]**.

The opposite angles in a parallelogram add up to 180° so you can pick any two angles as long as they total 180°.

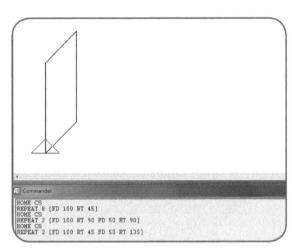

10

A rhombus can be drawn by changing the command to draw a parallelogram. The angles can stay the same, but the four sides need to be the same length. Can you work out how to draw a rhombus?

Check the picture if you need help.

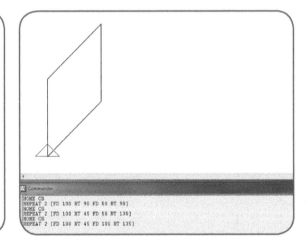

11

Now try changing the code to create different rhombuses of different sizes that have different angles. You don't need to save this activity.

Remember the two angles you use need to add up to 180°. Try **REPEAT 2 [FD 300 RT 100 FD 300 RT 80]** to get you started.

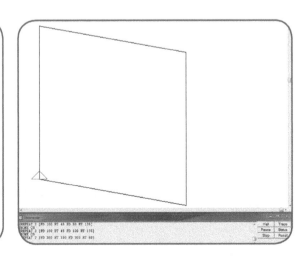

Now try this . . .

- Can you make all the shapes smaller by changing the forward command to **FD 50** instead of **FD 100**?

- What about making them bigger by increasing the lengths from 100 to 200?

- Can you write a single program to draw different-sized rectangles?

- Can you write the program for an octadecagon, which is a regular 18-sided shape?

 Work with a partner. Give them a magic pen, which can only do exactly what you tell them to do with it. Give them commands to draw different shapes. Can they follow procedures that use repetition in them so you don't have to keep repeating the same command?

Key words

Can you explain to a partner what these commands and words mean?

PD   **FD**   **RT**   **REPEAT**   **command**

How did you do?

Think about what you did in this activity. Did you:

- follow the steps to create programs that use repetition to draw a range of regular 2D shapes?

- change the programs to draw smaller shapes?

- change the programs to draw bigger shapes?

- write programs that draw different rectangles?

- work out the procedure needed to draw a regular 18-sided shape?

Activity 6: Logo
Writing nested programs

In the last activity, you used repetition in programs to draw different shapes. In this activity you will create programs that have a repetition command inside another repetition command. This is called nested repetition.

1

Start by typing **REPEAT 3 [REPEAT 3 [FD 100 RT 120] RT 120]** into the *Commander* bar. The program for drawing an equilateral triangle can be seen within another procedure for drawing an equilateral triangle. Press `Enter` to see what it draws.

Putting one repeat command into another is called nesting.

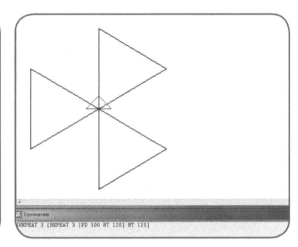

2

Now reset the screen (**HOME CS** and `Enter`) and begin to change the procedure by putting in the values for drawing a square. Type **REPEAT 4 [REPEAT 4 [FD 100 RT 90] RT 90]** into the *Commander* bar. Press `Enter` to see the repeating pattern using squares.

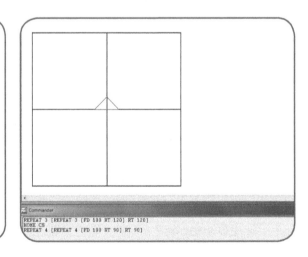

3

Now you are going to create a repeating pattern based on regular pentagons. Type **REPEAT 5 [REPEAT 5 [FD 100 RT 72] RT 72]** and press `Enter`.

Don't forget to reset the screen before starting a new pattern.

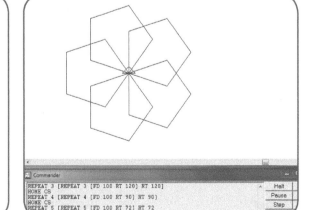

4

Can you work out what the procedure for drawing a similar repeating pattern based on regular hexagons would look like? Type **REPEAT 6 [REPEAT 6 [FD 100 RT 60] RT 60]** into the *Commander* bar and press Enter.

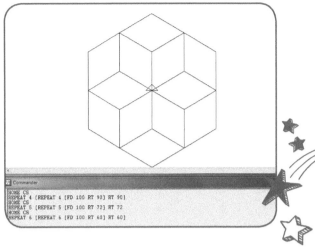

5

Next type **REPEAT 8 [REPEAT 8 [FD 100 RT 45] RT 45]** into the *Commander* bar and press Enter to draw a pattern created by repeating octagons.

> As this program contains eight sets of repetition, this gives us a clue that it will involve an octagon.

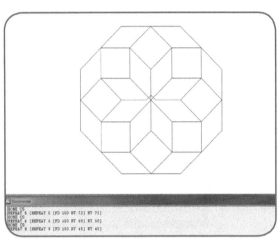

6

Change the program slightly and type **REPEAT 9 [REPEAT 9 [FD 50 RT 40] RT 40]**. Press Enter to see the nonagon repeating pattern.

> This time the FD command has been decreased from 100 to 50 so it fits more easily into the window.

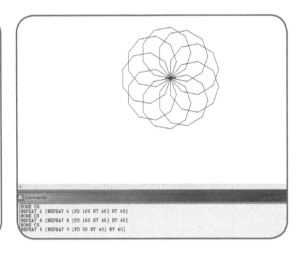

7

Type **REPEAT 10 [REPEAT 10 [FD 50 RT 36] RT 36]** into the *Commander* bar. Press Enter to see the repeating pattern.

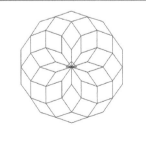

8

The command *BK* means move backwards. This can be used to create some interesting repeating patterns that don't rotate around a centre point. Try **REPEAT 6 [FD 40 REPEAT 6 [BK 40 RT 60]]**. Can you predict what shape will be repeated and what it will look like?

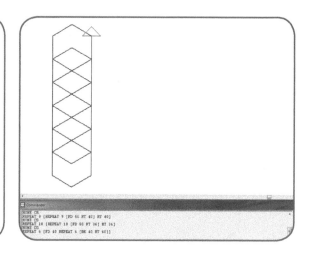

9

Can you change the program you created in step 8 so it repeats a square in a vertical line? What numbers will you need to change?

> Think about the number of angles a square has and the size of its external angles, which can be calculated by dividing 360 by its number of angles.

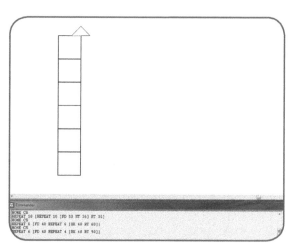

10

Read through the program **REPEAT 8 [REPEAT 4 [FD 50 RT 90] BK 50 RT 45]**. Can you work out what pattern it will draw? Try it out.

> Look at the amount of repetition – does this give you a clue?

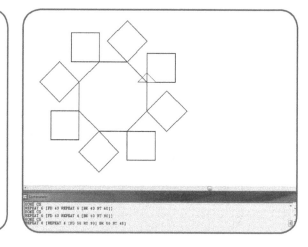

11

Can you change the program so it creates a similar pattern by repeating a triangle instead of a square? What values would need to change? Have fun exploring other patterns you can make by changing this program. You don't need to save this activity.

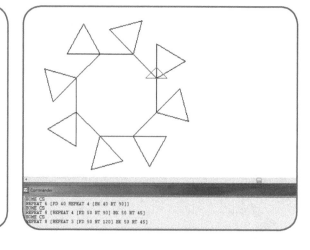

Now try this . . .

- Can you create a pattern based on repeating a regular pentadecagon, which is a 15-sided regular shape?

- Can you create a repeating pattern using an icosagon – a regular 20-sided shape?

- Can you change the procedure for the pentagon repeating pattern in step 3 to create a new repeating pattern? You could do this by doubling the number of times the shape is repeated and halving the angle of rotation.

- Can you create new repeating vertical patterns such as those in steps 8 and 9 by changing the shape that is repeated?

 Try creating repeating patterns by using 2D shape templates or perhaps cutting out shapes and creating a collage. Can you write instructions so a partner could reproduce your pattern without seeing it?

Key words

Can you explain to a partner what these words mean?

nesting   **procedure**   **repeating**   **program**   **command**

How did you do?

Think about what you did in this activity. Did you:

- write commands using nesting to create repeating patterns?

- create a program for a repeating pattern using a pentadecagon?

- create a repeating pattern using a icosagon?

- change the program in step 3 to create a new repeating pattern using pentagons?

- change the program in steps 8 and 9 to create a variety of repeating vertical patterns?

Activity 7: Logo
Creating and naming procedures

Now you will create and name your own procedure to produce a square. Once you have defined your own procedure, and the steps within it, you can program using it in the Commander bar just like any of the commands you have used so far. It can even be used within other procedures.

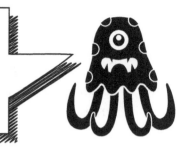

1

Let's start by seeing what Logo does when programmed to draw a square. Type **SQUARE** into the *Commander* bar and press `Enter`. Logo responds that it doesn't know how to draw a square.

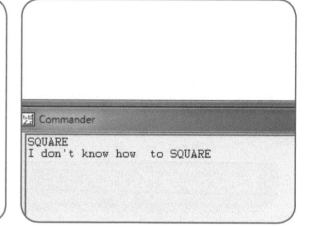

2

To define what you want Logo to do when you type in the command SQUARE, start by typing **TO SQUARE** into the *Commander* bar. This will bring up the *Input* window. Type in the instruction for drawing a square.

Remember that you used this in activity 1: **REPEAT 4 [FD 100 RT 90]**. This tells Logo to repeat the instructions in the brackets four times.

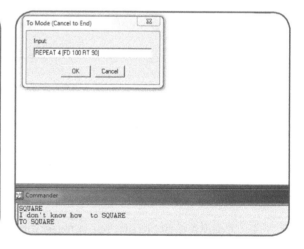

3

Click `OK` and then `Cancel`. Logo will now display *SQUARE defined*.

This means, you have described to Logo what you want it to do when you type SQUARE in the *Commander* bar.

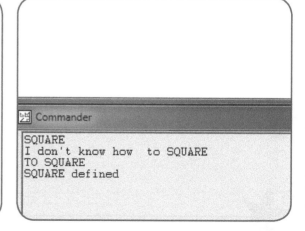

4

Now let's try out this new command that you have created. Type **SQUARE** into the *Commander* bar and press Enter. It should produce a square, just as you instructed it.

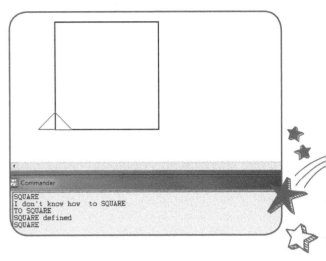

5

This new procedure can now be used just as you would use any of the other commands that have been built into Logo from the start. Let's try using your new command to create a pattern. Type **REPEAT 6 [SQUARE RT 60]** into the *Commander* bar, press Enter and watch what happens – can you predict what pattern this will produce?

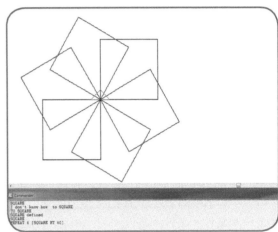

6

How about using your procedure in the definition of another procedure? Let's create a procedure to draw the above pattern and call it SQUAREPATTERN. Clear the screen. Type **TO SQUAREPATTERN** in the *Commander* bar and press Enter.

> When defining procedures, you always start with *TO* followed by the name of your procedure.

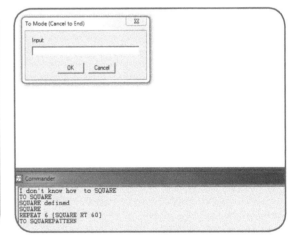

7

In the *Input* window, type in the command that you used to draw the pattern before: **REPEAT 6 [SQUARE RT 60]**. Then click OK and then Cancel. The procedure SQUAREPATTERN has now been defined.

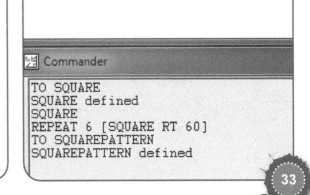

8

Try out your new procedure by typing **SQUAREPATTERN** in the *Commander* bar. What should happen when you press `Enter`? Try it out and see. If it doesn't produce your repeating square pattern again, you will need to go back to your code and do some debugging.

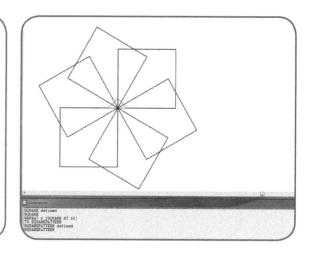

9

Now the procedure SQUAREPATTERN, which is based on another procedure (SQUARE), can be used as a command on its own. Remove the last pattern by clicking `Reset`. Type **REPEAT 6 [SQUAREPATTERN RT 30]** into the *Commander* bar. What will happen when you press `Enter`? Try it and see. You don't need to save this activity.

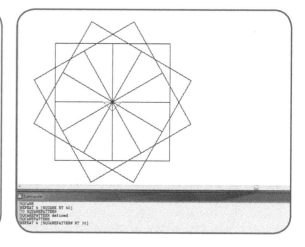

Now try this . . .

- Can you create other patterns using your procedure SQUAREPATTERN?

- Can you combine the two procedures, SQUARE and SQUAREPATTERN, to create a pattern?

- Can you define and create another procedure using the SQUARE procedure?

- Can you create procedures for a variety of 2D shapes and use them within other procedures?

 What patterns can you create by repeating 2D shapes?

Key words

Can you explain to a partner what these words mean?

command   **procedure**   **repetition**   **input**

How did you do?

Think about what you did in this activity. Did you:

- create a procedure that draws a square and then use that within another procedure?

- create other patterns using your SQUAREPATTERN procedure?

- combine the two procedures to create new patterns?

- create and define another procedure using the SQUARE procedure?

- create and define procedures that draw different 2D shapes and then use them within other procedures to create patterns?

Activity 8: Logo
Creating procedures using variables

In the last activity, you learned how to create and name procedures to carry out instructions. The first procedure you created was for drawing a square, but what if you want to produce a shape that changes size each time? This can be done by using variables in your procedure.

1

First let's remind ourselves of the procedure that we created to draw a square: REPEAT 4 [FD 100 RT 90]. By defining this as a procedure called SQUARE, Logo drew a square each time we entered the command SQUARE. Importantly, the square always had sides of 100 steps long because that's the length we have programmed into our procedure.

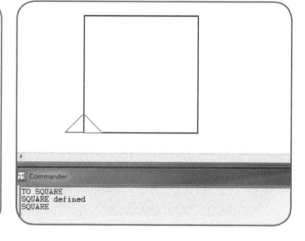

2

We are going to create a new square procedure. It will allow us to change the size of the square. To remove any old SQUARE procedures, close Logo and then open it up again. Type **TO SQUARE :N** in the *Commander* bar and press **Enter**.

N stands for the length of the sides of the square. N is a variable, which means it can be changed.

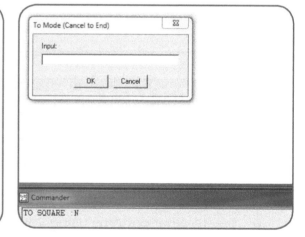

3

In the *Input* window, type in **REPEAT 4 [FD :N RT 90]**. Click **OK**, type in **END** and then click **OK** again.

You can see this looks really similar to our first SQUARE procedure except where it had the value '100' it now has :*N*. Remember *N* is a variable so this will allow us to change how many steps forward Logo should go each time.

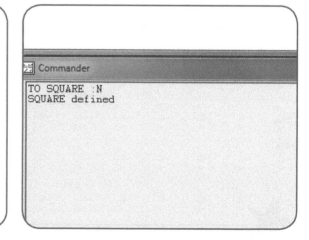

4

The procedure SQUARE has now been defined with a variable for the *move forward* value. Let's think about how we can now use this procedure. Type **SQUARE 200** into the *Commander* bar. What will happen when you press **Enter**? Try it and see.

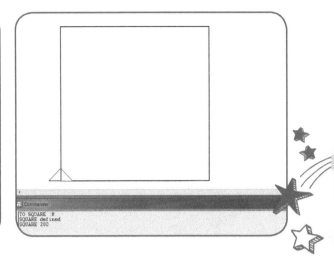

5

What happens when you type in **SQUARE 50** and press **Enter**? Try it.

The value you type in after the word *SQUARE* becomes the *FD* value in the procedure. What would you need to type in to create a square with sides of 75 steps?

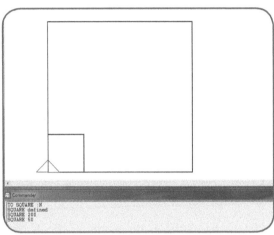

6

Can you create a procedure with one variable for the length of the sides and one variable for the number of sides? Type in **TO SHAPE :S :L** and press **Enter**.

S is the variable for the number of sides and *L* is the variable for the length of the sides. Variables can be called anything in Logo; you just need to remember the colon.

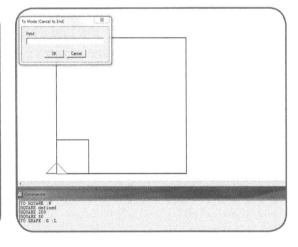

7

Now let's define our SHAPE procedure using the variables *S* and *L*. In the *Input* window, type **REPEAT :S [FD :L RT 360/:S]**. Logo will repeat the commands in the brackets as many times as the *S* value entered – the number of sides. The *move forward* value will be whatever *L* value is entered – the length of the sides.

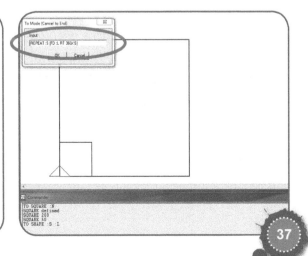

8

Click OK and then type in **END**. Click OK again. Let's use this procedure to draw a regular hexagon with sides of 100 steps. Press Reset to remove the squares. In the *Commander* bar, type in **SHAPE 6 100**. Press Enter to see what happens.

> Remember the *S* value comes first and is the number of sides. The length of the sides (the *L* value) comes second.

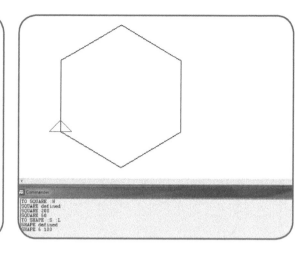

9

What regular shape will typing in **SHAPE 8 100** produce? Try it out.

> Keep checking back to the procedure *TO SHAPE :S :L* to help you predict.

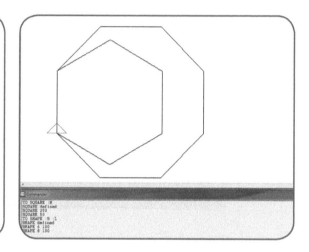

10

The command in the last step should have produced a regular octagon. If it didn't, take a look at your code and do some debugging to work out what went wrong. Now try adjusting the command to produce a smaller octagon. Type in **SHAPE 8 50** and press Enter.

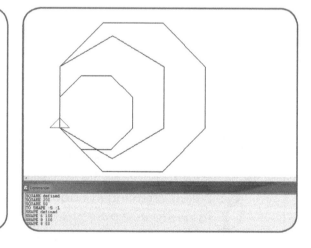

11

Can you predict how you would need to change the SHAPE procedure to produce a pentagon with sides of 25 steps? Type in **SHAPE 5 25** and see what happens.

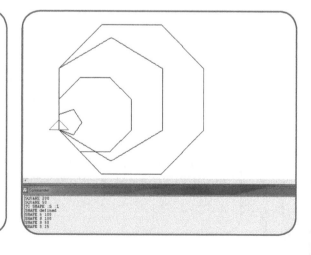

Now try this . . .

- Can you use the SHAPE procedure to draw a whole range of regular 2D shapes, such as a nonagon and decagon, in Logo?

- Can you produce a triangle using the SHAPE procedure? Can you create all types of triangle? Why not?

- Can you create a procedure that uses a variable *T* to produce triangles of different sizes?

- Can you create procedures that use variables to create repeating patterns of different sizes?

 Explore scaling regular shapes up and down in size. What measurements do you have to change each time?

Key words

Can you explain to a partner what these words mean?

command   **procedure**   **repeat**   **variable**

How did you do?

Think about what you did in this activity. Did you:

- create procedures using variables that allow you to draw shapes of different sizes and with different numbers of sides?

- use the SHAPE procedure to produce a range of regular 2D shapes?

- produce a triangle using the SHAPE procedure and work out why you can't produce all types of triangle?

- create a new procedure that uses the variable *T* to draw equilateral triangles of different sizes?

- create procedures that use variables to create repeating patterns of different sizes?

Activity 9: Snap! Converting text into sound

The Snap! activities are quite tricky but the resul[t] is great! Ask an adult to help if you get stuck.

Morse code is a method of sending messages as electronic pulses. The next four activities will explain how to program a text-to-Morse-code converter using Snap!. First you will create a procedure to convert Morse code text into a series of electronic sounds.

1

Start by typing **http://snap.berkeley.edu/snapsource/snap.html** into your web browser. On the left are the block palettes. You can drag and drop blocks into the scripting area, in the middle, to create scripts. On the top right is the stage where you can see your program in action when you run the script.

> Snap! looks similar to Scratch, but it allows you to build your own blocks.

2

As you are converting Morse code into electronic sounds, you will need blocks from the *Sound* palette. Click on `Sound` in the palette menu and drag a `set tempo to 60 bpm` block into the scripting area. Click inside the block, delete *60* and type in **500** to speed up the tempo.

> Tempo is the speed of a piece of music and is measured in 'bpm', which stands for beats per minute.

3

Next you are going to create a procedure to play Morse code. This means turning a script into one 'custom' block. Start by right-clicking in the scripting area and select `make a block`....

> Creating your own custom block allows you to use a script later without having to duplicate the whole thing again.

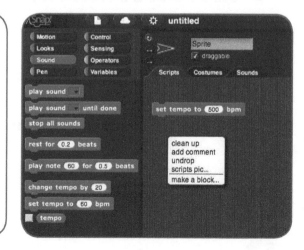

4

Now click on **Sound** in the *Make a block* window, as the block you are going to make is a sound block. Type in **Play Morse** as this is what the block is going to do. Click **OK**.

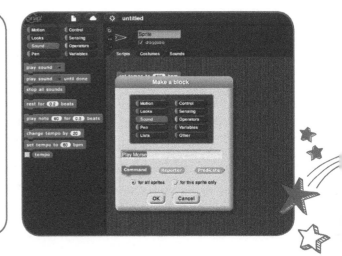

5

You should now see the *Block Editor* window. Click on the + sign on the right of your block to bring up the *Create input name* window. Then click on the ▶ symbol on the right to bring up a window with different types of input displayed. Choose **Text**, as the data you input into your Morse code converter will be text. In the box at the top, type in **Morse code** and click **OK**.

6

Now to work through the alphabet one character at a time. Click on the ⬚ symbol on the top left and select **import tools**. In the **Control** palette there will now be a **for i = 1 to 10** block. Drag it into the *Block Editor* and snap it onto your **Play Morse** block. The *i* in the **for i = 1 to 10** is a special variable, the iterator, which changes its value each time around the loop.

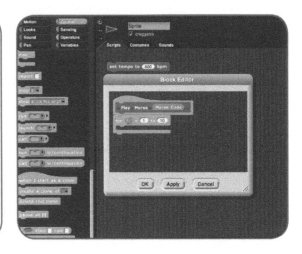

7

You need to edit the *10* because you don't know how long the Morse code is going to be, but you do want some sound played for each character. Click on the **Operators** palette and snap a **length of …** block into the **10** of the **for i = 1 to 10** block. Then click on your orange **Morse code** variable and drag and snap it into the **length of …** block.

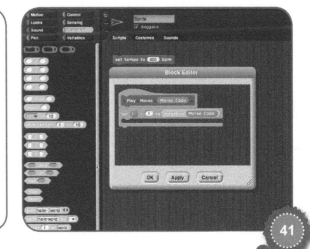

8

The procedure must identify if a character is a dot and what sound to play. On the `Control` palette snap an `if … else` block inside the `for i = 1 to 10`. Then click on the `Operators` palette and snap in an ☐ = ☐ block. Snap a `letter 1 of world` block into the first box. Drag an `i` and `Morse code` parameters from their blocks. Type a full stop (.) in the final box.

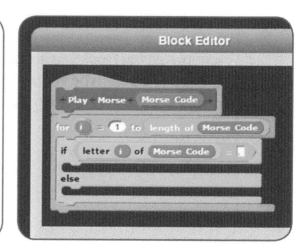

9

Now we need to tell it what sound to play. Click on the `Sound` palette and snap a `play note 60 for 0.5 beats` block underneath. Change *0.5* to **1**. A gap is needed between each character so snap on a `rest for 0.2 beats` block. Change *0.2* to **1**. This all means: read the characters in the Morse code string. If it is a dot, play note 60 for 1 beat, then rest for a beat.

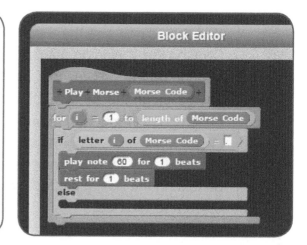

10

For the other characters, right-click on the `if … else` block and select `duplicate`. Snap the copied blocks underneath the `else` block. Change the *dot* to a *dash* (-) and *1* beat to **3** beats. Snap another `rest for 0.2 beats` block underneath *else*, changing it to **3** beats. What do you think this means?

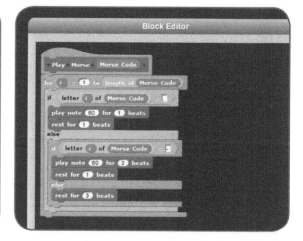

11

In the `Control` palette, find a `stop all` block. Change it to `this block` in the drop-down menu. Click `OK` and add it to the end of the script. Now click on the `Sound` palette and drag in the `Play Morse …` block. Type some Morse code (e.g. … --- …) into the block. Click on it to hear the Morse code. Save your project by clicking on the 🗋 icon.

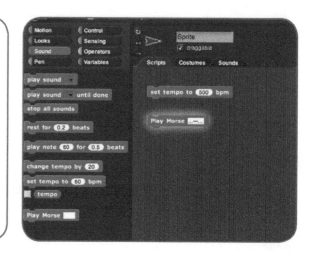

Now try this . . .

- Can you change the tempo of the sounds played?

- Can you change the sound?

- Can you make a bulb sprite light up with the Morse sound?

 Design an algorithm for a Morse decoder that could convert Morse code signals into dots and dashes. How easily could this be done in Snap!?

Key words

Can you explain to a partner what these words mean?

program **procedure** **input** **output** **parameter** **iteration** **iterator**

How did you do?

Think about what you did in this activity. Did you:

- create a procedure that converts text Morse code into sound?

- change the tempo of the sound produced?

- change the script to change the sound?

- add a bulb sprite that lights up with the Morse sound?

Activity 10: Snap! Converting text into Unicode

You have begun creating a text-to-Morse-code converter. You have created a procedure that turns text Morse code into sound. The next step is to create a function that converts a string of letters into a list of Unicode numbers. Computers store text as Unicode numbers.

1

Start by typing **http://snap.berkeley.edu/snapsource/snap.html** into your web browser. Click on the ▯ symbol on the top left and then on Open... to open the project that contains the *Play Morse* block that you created in the last activity.

2

First you are going to create another new *Operator* block. Right-click in the scripting area and select make a block.... In the *Make a block* window, click on Operators and call it **text as a list of Unicode**. This time click on Reporter. It is a reporter block because it is going to return the text to you as a list of numbers. Click OK.

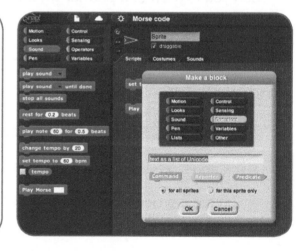

3

Now you should see the *Block Editor* window. Click on the second + sign in the block to bring up the *Create input name* window. Type in **text**. Then click on the ▶ symbol on the right and select Text in the display of input types that has now been brought up in the window. Click OK. This tells the block that the input will be text.

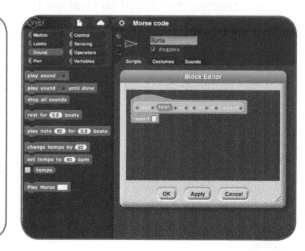

4

Drag the `report` block away from the one above it so they disconnect. Now click on the `Variables` palette and snap a grey `script variables` block underneath the top block. Click on `a` and type **Unicode** in the *Script variable name* window. Click `OK`.

> The *report* block is there because when the function is run, it has to return a value to the main Snap! program.

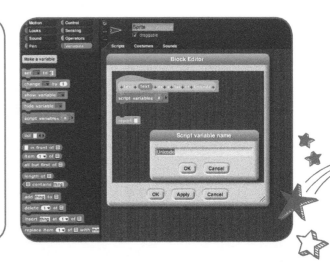

5

Now you are going to set the *Unicode* variable to be an empty list to start with. Snap a `set ... to 0` block underneath. Select `Unicode` in the drop-down menu in the block. Then snap a `list ...` block into the *0* of the `set ... to 0` block. Click on the ◄ symbol in the *list* block to remove the white box.

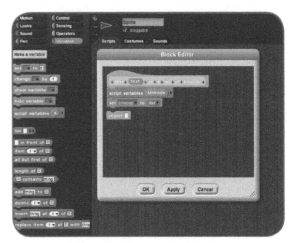

6

As in activity 9, we will use a `for i = 1 to 10` iteration block to work its way through all the text that has been input into the function. Click on the `Control` palette and snap a `for i = 1 to 10` block underneath. As before, from the `Operators` palette select the `length of ...` block and the orange `text` parameter from above (see right).

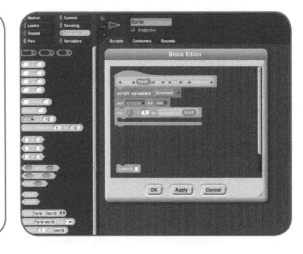

7

Click on the `Variables` palette and insert an `add thing to ...` variable block inside your `for i = 1 to 10` block. Click on the `Unicode` variable in the `script variables` block and drag and insert into the *list* block ▤ of `add thing to ...`.

> This will add something new to the end of the *Unicode* list that our function returns.

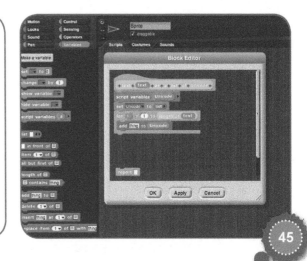

8

Next we need to add on the Unicode of the next character in the text. To do this, click on the `Operators` palette and insert a `Unicode of …` block into the `add thing to … Unicode` block where it says *thing*. Then snap a `letter 1 of world` block into the box that says *a*. Snap in an orange `i` variable where it says *1* and `text` parameter where it says *world*.

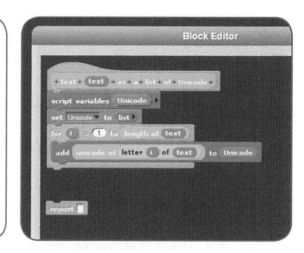

9

Now snap the `report` block back onto the end of the script and snap a `Unicode` variable inside it. Then click OK.

This is needed because we want to tell the function to report a list of Unicode back. The user could type in text and get a list of Unicode back.

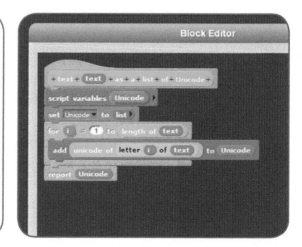

10

To test your function you need to add the new block to the scripting area, so click on the `Operators` palette and drag a `text … as a list of Unicode` block into the scripting area. Type some text into the block. Try **hello**.

Remember we set the input as text. If your function works correctly, what should the output be?

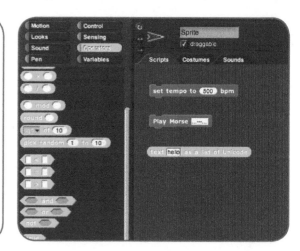

11

Finally, click on the `text … as a list of Unicode` block to run it. It should convert the text you typed into Unicode. Be sure to save your project again.

Remember Unicode is what computers use to represent letters. We can see that a lower case 'h' is 104 in Unicode and so on. The output produced by your function is Unicode.

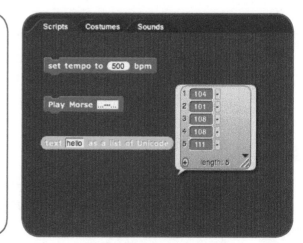

Now try this . . .

- Can you type **HELLO** in upper case into your block? What do you notice about the Unicode? Do upper and lower case letters have the same Unicode number? How are these related?

- Can you type more than one word with spaces in between into your block? What is the Unicode number for a space?

- Can you find out the Unicode numbers for all letters of the alphabet?

- How are numbers and other characters, like non-Latin alphabets, represented in Unicode?

 How quickly can you convert words in text to their equivalents in Unicode?

Key words

Can you explain to a partner what these words mean?

function   input   output   variable   list   parameter   Unicode

How did you do?

Think about what you did in this activity. Did you:

- build a block that converts text into Unicode?

- explore upper case and lower case letters in Unicode?

- find out how a space is represented in Unicode?

- find out the Unicode numbers for the whole alphabet?

- explore how numbers are represented in Unicode?

Activity 11: Snap!
Using the list lookup function

So far you have built a block that converts Morse code text into sounds and another block that converts text into Unicode. Now you need to convert Unicode numbers into Morse code (dots and dashes) one character at a time using a function block.

1 Start by typing **http://snap.berkeley.edu/snapsource/snap.html** into your web browser. Click on the ◻ symbol on the top left and then on Open... to open your Morse code converter project. You will be building on this in this activity.

2 Right-click in the scripting area and select make a block.... Click on Operators as this will be an operator block. Type in a name that explains what the block does, such as **Unicode as Morse**. As in the last activity, click on Reporter and OK. This is a reporter block because it is going to return a list of Morse code to the main program.

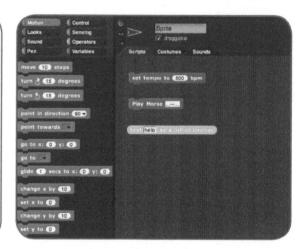

3 In the *Block Editor*, click on the + sign to the right of the word *Unicode* to bring up the *Create input name* window. Type in **Unicode** as this will be the input into the function. Then click on the ▶ symbol on the right to bring up the input types. This time select Number. Unicode is made up of numbers so the function needs to expect numbers as input. Click OK.

4

Disconnect the `report` block. We are going to make a new temporary script variable to use inside this function, so click on the `Variables` palette and snap on a `script variables` block. Click on the `a` block inside it and type in **Morse**. Click `OK`. Morse code will be returned at the end of the procedure so drag the `Morse` variable block into the report block for later.

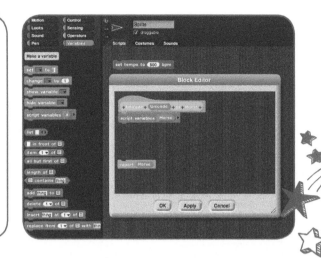

5

Add another *script variables* block and change the *a* to **Morse code**. We need to set the Morse code lookup table to be a long list of what Morse code looks like so add a `set … to 0` block – choose `Morse code` from its menu, then snap in a `list …` block instead of 0.

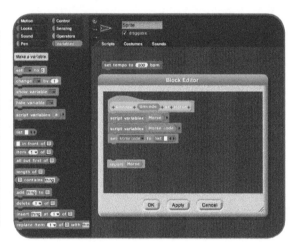

6

To set the lookup table for each letter of the alphabet, click on the right-hand arrow in the list block until there are 26 white boxes. Type the Morse code for each letter of the alphabet in each box, e.g. A is .- and so on. The whole alphabet is here: **http://morsecode.scphillips.com/morse2.html**.

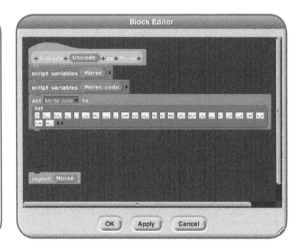

7

Now to match Unicode numbers to the Morse code in the list. From the `Control` palette, get an `if … else` block. Click on `Operators` and snap an `and` block into the `if … else` block. Snap a ☐ > ☐ block in the first box and a ☐ < ☐ block in the second. Snap in `Unicode` variables as shown and set the limits to **64** and **91**. This sets the lower case letters.

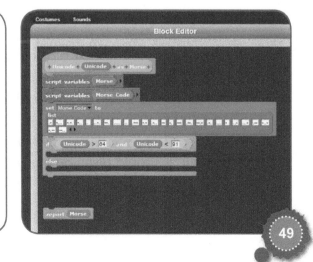

8

From the `Variables` palette, add a `set ... to ...` block and choose `Morse` from the menu. Snap in an `item ... of ...` block instead of the 0. Add a $\bigcirc - \bigcirc$ block (`Operators` palette) into the *item* block and then snap a `Unicode` block inside its first box. Type **64** in the second. Snap a `Morse code` variable in the other box.

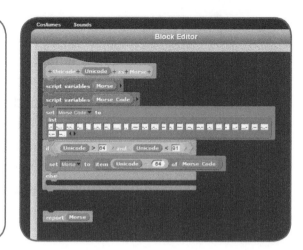

9

Right-click on the `if ... else` block to duplicate it and snap the copy under *else*. Change the numbers so the limits are **95** and **124** and we subtract **96** to set the upper case letters. For all other characters, set the Morse code to a space. Add a `set ... to ...` block (from `Variables`) in the *else* section. Choose `Morse` in its menu and type a `space` in the white box.

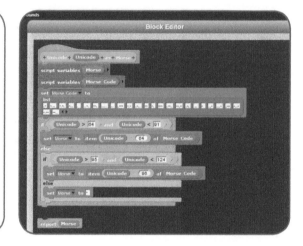

10

To make sure the Morse code has a space between each string of dots and dashes, add a `set ... to ...` block before the *report* block. Choose `Morse` from its drop-down menu, then add a `join` block from the `Operators` palette. Snap a `Morse` block into the first box in the *join* block and type in a space into the second box. Snap the `report` block back in place.

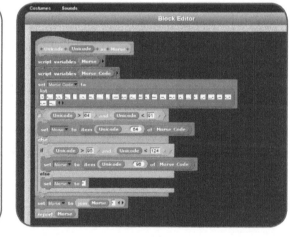

11

Test your block: click `OK` and drag your `Unicode ... as Morse` block into the scripting area. Use your `text ... as a list of Unicode` block to find out the Unicode of a letter such as 'z', which is 122. Then type **122** into your new block and double-click it. It should give you --.. which is the Morse code of 'z'. Save your project.

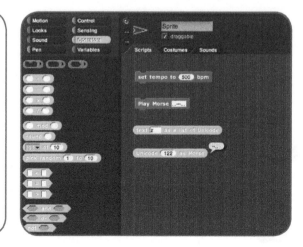

Now try this . . .

- Can you try out upper and lower case versions of the same letter? Do they produce the same Morse code?

- What happens when you type a space?

- Can you work out the Unicode for a word such as *hello* and then convert that into Morse code?

- Can you convert two words? Is there a space between them when they are converted into Morse code?

 How could you change your block to communicate in a secret version of Morse code?

Key words

Can you explain to a partner what these words mean?

function   **input**   **output**   **variable**   **parameter**   **Unicode**

How did you do?

Think about what you did in this activity. Did you:

- create a function that converts Unicode into Morse code?

- convert upper and lower case Unicode letters and find that the Morse code is the same?

- convert a space into Morse code?

- convert a whole word from Unicode into Morse code?

- convert a phrase from Unicode into Morse code?

Activity 12: Snap!
Combining functions and procedures

You have created three custom blocks: a procedure to play Morse code as sound, a function to convert text to Unicode and another function to convert Unicode to Morse code. The final task is to combine these to create a program that will convert a string of text into Morse code and play it back as a sound.

1 Start by typing **http://snap.berkeley.edu/snapsource/snap.html** into your web browser. Click on the symbol on the top left and then on `Open…` to open your Morse code converter project. You will be building on this in this activity.

2 Start by making a new string variable. Click on the `Variables` palette and then `Make a variable`. Type in **string** and click `OK`. Let's start by setting the string to something easy to begin with, like the word *hello*. Add a `set … to 0` block to the scripting area and choose `string` in the drop-down menu. Type **hello** into the white box.

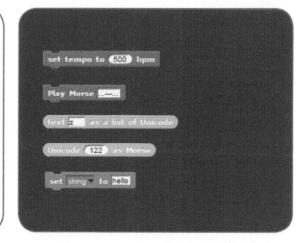

3 This string of text (the word *hello*) needs to be turned into a list of Unicode values. Create another variable called **Unicode**. Then snap another `set … to 0` block underneath and choose *Unicode* from its drop-down menu. Snap in a `text … as a list of Unicode` block (from `Operators`) and `string` block (from `Variables`) as shown.

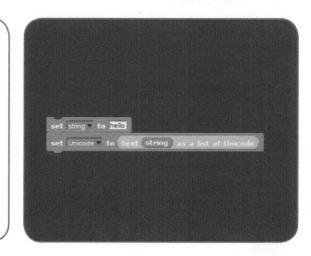

4

Test it by clicking on the `set string to hello` variable block. What do you think will happen? It should turn the word *hello* into a list of Unicode numbers, as shown. If it doesn't, you need to go back and debug your code.

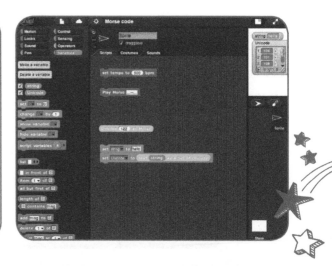

5

Now to produce the Morse code one character at a time from that Unicode list. Make a new variable called **Morse**. Add a `set ... to` block and choose `Morse` from the menu. Set it to an empty string by deleting the *0* in the white box. Then you will work one step at a time through the Unicode list.

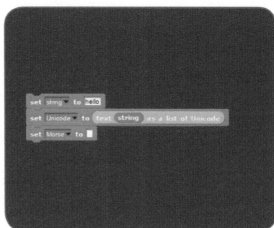

6

Click on the `Control` palette and add a `for i = 1 to 10` iteration block, which you have used before. Go back to the `Variables` palette and snap a `length of ...` block into the last box of the `for i = 1 to 10` block and snap a `Unicode` variable block into that.

This means it will work its way through the length of the Unicode list, one number at a time.

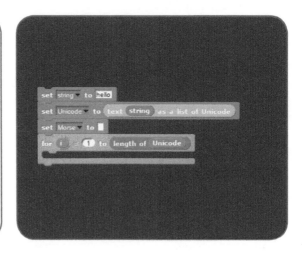

7

Snap a `set ... to 0` block in the `for i = 1 to 10` block. Choose `Morse` in its menu. Then click on the `Operators` palette and snap a `join` block inside it. Snap a `Morse` variable and `Unicode ... as Morse` function (from the scripting area) inside the `i` block. This programs each new Morse character to join whatever is in the Morse string already.

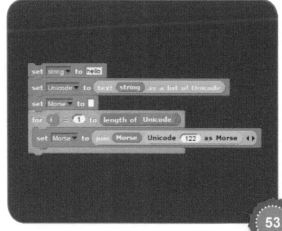

53

8

Now you need to add an `item … of …` block (from `Variables`) into the `Unicode as Morse` block. Where it says *1*, drag and snap in an `i` variable (from the *for i…* block) and then snap in a `Unicode` variable where the *list* symbol is.

> Remember, this means it will go through the list one number at a time and add on the Morse to our Morse string.

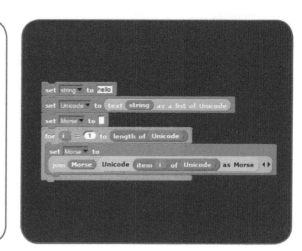

9

Time to test your program so far again. Click on the top `set … to 0` block to run it. It should convert the text string (*hello*) into a list of Unicode values and then work its way through that Unicode list, turning it into Morse code one number at a time.

> You can see the Morse string at the bottom of the stage area. This is the word *hello* represented in Morse code.

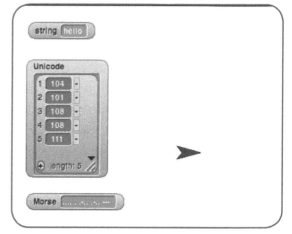

10

The final step of the program is to play the Morse code back as a sound. So, snap your `Play Morse` block from activity 9 onto the end of your script. Then snap a `Morse` variable inside it.

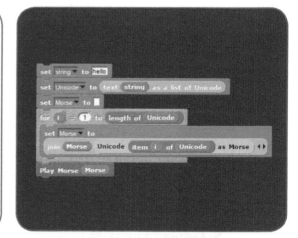

11

You can now test your finished text to Morse code converter. Run the final script by double-clicking on it. As well as converting text into Morse code characters, it should also play this Morse code back to you as electronic pulses.

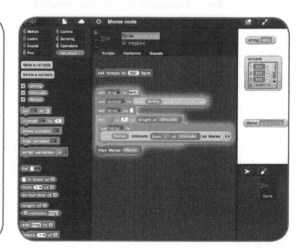

Now try this . . .

- Can you try out the word *HELLO* in upper case? Does it produce and play back the same Morse code as the lower case?

- Can you try another word like *SOS*?

- Can you type in a phrase to test how it deals with spaces between words?

- Are there any text strings that don't work? Could you extend the program so it can deal with Morse for digits and punctuation?

 Try working through all the steps your Morse code converter goes through. How quickly can you convert text into Morse code and then play it back as a sound? How could you produce short and long pulses to represent the dots and dashes?

Key words

Can you explain to a partner what these words mean?

program   **function**   **procedure**   **variable**   **input**   **output**   **list**   **iteration**   **Unicode**

How did you do?

Think about what you did in this activity. Did you:

- combine the different custom blocks to create a program that converts text into Morse code that it plays back?

- test upper and lower case versions of the same word?

- try out different words?

- try out phrases?

- extend the program so it can deal with Morse for digits and punctuation?

Glossary

- **Action:** the process of doing an operation or following an instruction.

- **Command:** an instruction given to an object or character to make something happen.

- **Consequence:** the result or effect of doing an operation or following an instruction.

- **Debug:** to find and get rid of errors within code.

- **Do** [in Kodu]: what your object must 'perform' or do as the result of a command (see 'When [in Kodu]').

- **FD** [in Logo]: the command used to move Logo forward, followed by a numerical value to set the distance moved, e.g. FD 40.

- **Function:** a small section of code that makes a specific process happen, and importantly returns a result (or answer).

- **Input:** information given to a computer to make something happen, e.g. a number, a mouse click or button press.

- **Iteration:** the repetition of a command based on the result from the last time the command was used.

- **Iterator:** an object that allows the user to work through a list.

- **List:** a series of connected items.

- **Nesting:** to embed (put) an object inside another, e.g. nesting functions within a spreadsheet.

- **Output:** something that a computer produces when given an instruction, e.g. a number, an on-screen image, a sound or vibration.

- **Parameter:** an amount that can be set by a user.

- **Path:** this allows you to create a 'journey' for your graphic within a piece of software.

- **PD** [in Logo]: pen down; the command used to instruct Logo to 'draw' on the screen. What is drawn is set by the other commands input by the user.

- **Procedure:** a small section of code that makes a specific process happen.

- **Program:**
  1. a sequence of instructions written to perform a task or solve a problem, using a programming language (noun)
  2. to create or change a program (verb).

- **REPEAT** [in Logo]: the command used to instruct Logo to carry out a command again, or for a certain number of times, e.g. REPEAT 25.

- **Repeat:** take a command (or set of commands) and follow its instruction again (and again).

- **Repeating:** something that happens again and again, such as a command or a pattern.

- **Repetition:** the act of repeating something: following an instruction again (and again).

- **RT** [in Logo]: the command used to turn Logo right, followed by the angle to turn, e.g. RT 45 means 'turn to the right 45 degrees'.

- **Test:** to run the program or set of commands to check how well (if at all) the code works.

- **Unicode:** a computing language that is used to represent characters as numbers.

- **User:** the person who uses a program or application.

- **Variable:** a piece of data that changes or can be changed.

- **When** [in Kodu]: the command your object must follow for an action to be performed (see 'Do [in Kodu]').